THE TOP PERFORMER'S GUIDE TO ATTITUDE

BY TIM URSINY, PhD,
GARY DeMOSS, &
MARC A. YBABEN, PhD

SOURCEBOOKS, INC.
NAPERVILLE, ILLINOIS

Published by Sourcebooks, Inc.
P.O. Box 4410, Naperville, Illinois 60567-4410
(630) 961-3900
Fax: (630) 961-2168
www.sourcebooks.com

Library of Congress Cataloging-in-Publication Data

Ursiny, Timothy E.
  The top performer's guide to attitude / by Tim Ursiny, Gary Demoss & Marc A.
Ybaben.
     p. cm.
  ISBN 978-1-4022-1036-5 (hbk.)
  1. Employees--Attitudes. 2. Employee motivation. I. DeMoss, Gary. II. Ybaben,
Marc A. III. Title.
  HF5549.5.M63U77 2007
  658.3'14--dc22

                                    2007035832

Printed and bound in the United States of America.
BG 10 9 8 7 6 5 4 3 2 1

ACKNOWLEDGMENTS

As always we thank Dominique Raccah, Peter Lynch, Todd Stocke, Erin Nevius, Sarah Riley, Dojna Shearer, and all of our wonderful friends at Sourcebooks. They treat us well.

Special thanks to Lisa Kueng, whose keen editorial comments helped mold this book.

Thanks to Zachary Ursiny and Jorden Bennett for their research on top performers and stories of unbreakable attitudes. Thanks also to Colton Ursiny for his tenacity and research on historical figures.

DEDICATION

From Tim:

For my mother, Frances Knight.

From Gary:

To my wonderful wife, Laurelyn, and to my children, Brandon, Matt, Jonathan, Leah, Lauren, and Tyler.

From Marc:

To my family, Rose, Conner, and Carina, for their endless support and for making sure my attitude is in the right place!

CONTENTS

INTRODUCTION

WHY TOP PERFORMERS FOCUS ON ATTITUDE

The greatest discovery of any generation is that a human being can alter his life by altering his attitude.

—Psychologist William James

Impossible is a word only to be found in the dictionary of fools.

—Napoleon

Be careful, because this book could change your life! Does that seem like an outrageous claim? Can a book truly change your life? It can if you approach your reading with the right attitude. Former United States President Woodrow Wilson said,

We grow great by dreams. All big men are dreamers. They see things in the soft haze of a spring day or in the red fire of a long winter's evening. Some of us let these great dreams die, but others nourish and protect them; nurse them through bad days till they bring them to the sunshine and light which comes always to those who sincerely hope that their dreams will come true.

Some men and women are afraid to dream. After all, if you dream and your dream doesn't come true, you may look like a fool (or just think you look like a fool—the two things can be indistinguishable from one another). If you dream, you may fail. If you dream, then you risk disappointment. So what is the argument for dreaming? The one we find most compelling is summarized in a quote from Victor Hugo, the famous French novelist: "There is nothing like a dream to create the future."

Dreamers change the future. They influence their future, and many times they can even impact the world. All of us are gifted with abilities that give us an incredible amount of influence over our lives and the lives of others. Some hide or bury these talents and deprive the world, while others use their abilities fully and bring about amazing changes.

Those who refuse to dream sabotage their future and waste their gifts. They toss away their dreams and live a life less than what they could have had. Sure there are risks to dreaming, but so what? Disappointment is only disappointment; it is only torturous if we allow it to be. Failure is only a chance to learn something. People who call us fools are just mocking us—it doesn't mean anything! It does not have any power in and of itself. You don't need to be hurt by mocking, and you don't even need to be angered by it. If anything, feel compassion for those who are so stuck and afraid to dream that they have to bring down true dreamers in order to feel safe. The power you give to disappointment, failure, and other people's opinions is your choice.

The basic premise of this book is that attitude is a choice. And although there are many wonderful books that focus on attitude, few (if any) really lay out the choices that you can make with your mind, heart, and behaviors that will produce the attitude of a top performer. This book is about blocking and tackling. What are the attitudes to put aside (before they take control), and what are the attitudes to nurture so that they grow and overwhelm you with joy? Choosing to be positive is the choice that encompasses all other choices. Buckingham and Clifton, the authors of *Now, Discover Your Strengths*, list positivity as one of the strengths that someone can bring to the workplace. Based on a Gallup study of over two million people, they say this about individuals with the strength of positivity:

- "You are generous with praise, quick to smile, and always on the lookout for the positive in the situation."
- " . . . people want to be around you. Their world looks better around you because your enthusiasm is contagious."
- "You find ways to make everything more exciting and more vital."

- "Somehow you can't quite escape your conviction that it is good to be alive, that work can be fun, and that no matter what the setbacks, one must never lose one's sense of humor."

Positivity is the overwhelming choice for a top-performing attitude, and within this one choice there are many other choices. This book is about those choices that will impact your attitude. They are presented here in three categories:

1. Choices about yourself. How do you view yourself and your personal power? How do you treat yourself?
2. Choices you make about others. How do you view and interact with friends, coworkers and family members, and how does that relate to being a top performer?
3. Choices about how you relate to the world. How do you see and react to the world and its unique challenges?

We realize these categories have some overlap, and certainly one could argue that some of these questions are applicable for more than one of these categories. But why argue? This is a book on positive attitude, so let's start out on the right foot! As you read, make sure to keep your eye on the big picture. These choices intersect and build on each other. For example, some people may view our writings on choosing to be tenacious and choosing to embrace those things you can't control as contradictory. They are not. If you read carefully, you will discover how these relate. After examining your choices we will walk you through a step-by-step process for taking your attitude to the next level.

To provide consistency, each chapter is made up of the following components:

- **Attitude Adages:** Quotes are sprinkled throughout the book, and we will start each chapter with two quotes that we feel capture the spirit of that chapter.

- **In a Nutshell:** Here we will present a brief summary of what you can expect in the chapter.

- **It's All in How You Look at It:** This segment is the main substance of the chapter. We will review stories, research, lessons, and historical examples of top-performing attitudes. Please note that when we share personal stories we will use "I" instead of identifying which author is speaking for the sake of simplicity.

- **Interviews with Top Performers:** We interviewed top performers and asked them questions about the attitudes, habits, and behaviors that helped create

TIM URSINY, PhD, GARY DeMOSS, & MARC A. YBABEN, PhD

their success, along with how they nurture a positive attitude in others. In this section, we briefly summarize their insights.

- **Putting It into Practice:** The last segment in each chapter will suggest exercises for taking your attitude to the next level. Do not skip these! They are likely the most important part of every chapter.

Are you ready to dream? Are you ready to believe that a little book can have a huge impact on your life? Are you ready to take that chance? If so, then you are ready to find out what top performers know about attitude.

SECTION I

INVESTMENT
IN ATTITUDE

CHAPTER 1

WHAT TOP PERFORMERS KNOW ABOUT ATTITUDE

Attitude Adages

A happy person is not a person in a certain set of circumstances, but rather a person with a certain set of attitudes.

—Telecaster Hugh Downs

Finally, brothers, whatever is true, whatever is noble, whatever is right, whatever is pure, whatever is lovely, whatever is admirable—if anything is excellent or praiseworthy—think about such things.

—The apostle Paul, in his letter to the Philippians
(Philippians 4:8)

In a Nutshell

We will start this chapter with what appears to be a sob story (don't worry, it's not), and then we will explore this elusive thing called *attitude*. What is it? Why does it have such power? What can a top-performing attitude really, truly do for you on a practical level? We will look at how attitude functions, and how some people who have no right to remain optimistic choose to be optimistic anyway. We will also present research and expert opinions on the role attitude plays in happiness, performance, and teams. This is the last chapter for any naysayers. After reading this research you must either decide to jump in with both feet or go buy a different book! We end the chapter with a quiz to test how your attitude compares to the attitude that gives top performers the ability to make things happen.

It's All in How You Look at It

Some would say that I don't come from a particularly wonderful childhood. My parents divorced for the second time when I was in eighth grade, and we kids had to choose which parent to live with. I chose my mother because we were closer and, quite frankly, I thought she needed me more. We moved into government subsidized housing and were surrounded by drug users and dealers. This was a shock to me because I was a pastor's kid who had grown up in many small towns and was somewhat naive to the ways of the world. I would go to school (already depressed by my parents' divorce and missing my friends) only to get picked on daily by larger kids who sensed my weakness. We were challenged financially, and I was on the free lunch program at school. In order not to shame us, they had a secret code—we simply winked at the cashier until she learned who we were. Momentarily, kids at school thought I was really sly and was just getting out of paying for my lunch. Innocently, I gave them the real reason. You can imagine how that went over. One particular day when I was 15, after being beaten up, forced to sit in others' spit, and ridiculed by a gang of kids, I found myself sitting in my darkened bedroom questioning if my life was always going to be so difficult. The thought of a life full of such embarrassment and pain was almost overwhelming. Fortunately, as I sat on my bed struggling with my future, I realized that I was asking the wrong question. "Will my life always be like this?" assumed that I was a passive participant. What if I could decide differently? What if I could decide that I was going to have a happy life instead of a sad one? I started saying such things to myself as, "It doesn't have to be like this," "This is not the right path for me," and "I can change this." At that crucial decision point I decided to trust that things could get better, and even if they did not get better, I could. Despite the facts of my life I decided to take an attitude of optimism, and that attitude is a huge part of what has made me who I am today.

Although those days were challenging, I rarely look back on them as bad. They were so much a part of my development that I see them as the gauntlet that I had to walk through to sharpen my perspective and skills rather than a burden to carry the rest of my life. What got me through those times was a simple belief: It will all work out. This belief was challenged a few times, and to be honest, I did have doubts on a few occasions. But most of the time I just believed that things would be okay if I hung in there long enough and wisely enough. And I was right!

Today I love life. It has its imperfections, but the majority of the time I just feel grateful. I feel thankful for my family, my friends, my work, and often I even feel grateful for the tough times. I feel this because of that choice and subsequent choices to be positive and optimistic. Top performers know that attitude is a choice. Although a few people seem to have been born with an incredible attitude, most of us have had to choose how we view ourselves, others, and the world. This book is based on the premise that you are able to choose your attitude.

What Is Attitude?

I heard a mother in the grocery store the other day say to her 6-year-old, "Don't give me any attitude." What in the world does that mean? What is this attitude thing that we are so concerned about? Oh, we know it when we see it. When someone is "giving us attitude" we can definitely feel it (and usually don't like it because it is a negative attitude). On the other hand, most of us love someone with a genuinely positive attitude. Now, we are not talking about the person who just pretends to have a great attitude, but rather individuals who you enjoy being around because they are so inspiring and uplifting. This type of person is well-loved, memorable, and effective and gets the job done. This person is a top performer.

Taking a quick look into a thesaurus, you will find the following words related to attitude:

- Approach
- Outlook
- Feelings
- Mind-set
- Posture

The Merriam-Webster Online Dictionary adds more to this list, defining attitude as

1. "A position assumed for a specific purpose"
2. "A mental position with regard to a fact or state"
3. "A feeling or emotion toward a fact or state"

Mind, Heart, and Body

These definitions tell us that attitude is related to your entire being. It is how you think, how you feel, and how you act. Attitude represents that connection between mind, heart, and body. For that reason, we are not going to just focus on what you are saying to yourself. Rather, we will attempt to help you align your entire mind-set as well as your feelings and actions with those of top performers. And if you let us, we will help you continue to grow your freedom from the negative influences that exist in the world.

Conceptually, if we think of attitude as the whole package of the individual, we can demonstrate the flow with the following chart, The Flow of Attitude.

Figure 1: The Flow of Attitude

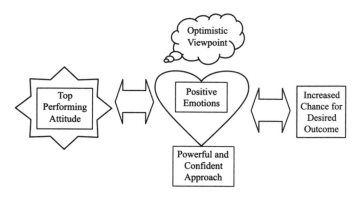

Thoughts, feelings, and behaviors all flow together, and each impacts the other two. In our chart, a top-performing attitude produces an optimistic viewpoint and positive emotions, and it leads to a confident approach to the situation. An optimistic attitude + positive emotions + a confident approach = far greater chances for a desired outcome. Attitude will determine what you see in the world, how you will interpret what you see, and how you react to what you interpret. Attitude is like the filter on your furnace. A great attitude will screen out the dirt and only allow the clear air to go through. Oh, you know the dirt is out there; you know that it endangers your health to let dust flow unfettered through your mind. You also know that just as a positive attitude increases your chances for desired outcomes, the reverse is also true. Getting results increases your positive thoughts, emotions, and behaviors, which creates a better attitude. It is all intertwined, and it all flows.

The Impact of Attitude

Best-selling author Barbara Sher said, "Imaginary obstacles are insurmountable. Real ones aren't." Attitude has a huge impact on your life, happiness, health, work performance, sales, teams, management, and so forth. In a March 2007 article entitled "The Progenitors of Positivity," *Newsweek* tracks a focus on attitude back to Phineas Quimby, who in the mid-1800s claimed that every human disease could be cured in the mind. The article also traces the following individuals as the early proponents of positive attitude:

- Wallace Wattles, who wrote *The Science of Getting Rich* in 1910
- Emile Coue, who developed a therapy style based on positive self-talk in the early twentieth century
- Charles Fillmore, who wrote *The Twelve Powers of Man* in the 1930s, which focuses on the power of the mind

- Norman Vincent Peale, who wrote the best-selling *The Power of Positive Thinking* in 1952

The list goes on, but the point is that focusing on positive attitude is not new. It has been around for a long time and continues to fascinate us as we learn more and more about the power of the human thought process. Researchers have shown the power of attitude in multiple areas.

Happiness

In *The 100 Simple Secrets of Happy People*, David Niven summarizes several research studies that demonstrate that external situations and events do not control our happiness.

- Chen (1996) revealed that attitude is a much better predictor of happiness than the number of good and bad events you have been through.
- Sirgy, Cole, Kosenko, and Meadow (1995) revealed that "People who have the most are only as likely to be as happy as those who have the least. People who like what they have, however, are twice as likely to be as happy as those who actually have the most."

This research is crucial to our premise that your attitude is your choice, and that this choice will have a dramatic impact on your life. It supports the fact that attitude creates happiness much more than life circumstances do.

Dealing with Organizational Change

In 1999, Judge and his colleagues explored how personality factors and attitudes influence coping abilities during difficult organizational transitions. They found that the success of new processes and other changes was directly related to the attitudes of the individuals within the organization. These attitudes included the belief that these individuals had control over their lives, the willingness to take risks, openness to new experiences, self-confidence, tolerance for ambiguity, and a generally positive demeanor.

Combating Anxiety

Poor stress tolerance and anxiety have a negative impact on performance and attitude. The figure below, adapted from *Mastery of Your Anxiety and Worry*, by Barlow, Craske, and O'Leary demonstrates this relationship further.

The main point of this illustration is to show that attitudes, physical symptoms, and behaviors all have the ability to negatively impact each other. Intervening on any level will have an impact; therefore, attitude can be the antidote for anxiety in the form of our thoughts, emotions, and behaviors.

Figure 2: How our attitudes interact with our behaviors and our bodies.

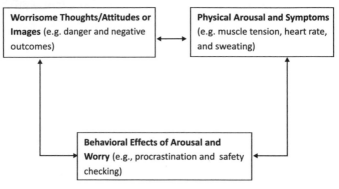

Hardiness

In a *Consulting Psychology Journal* article entitled, "The Hardy Organization: Success by turning change to advantage," Maddi, Khoshaba and Pammenter explore the concept of hardiness for individuals. They describe it as a set of attitudes and skills that allow an individual to handle stress, disruptive changes, or chronic conflicts. They describe three "HardiAttitudes"—commitment, control, and challenge. Those strong in *commitment* have the attitude that involvement with tasks, people, and contexts creates meaningful purpose in life. Those strong in *control* believe that you can influence your circumstances through personal struggle. People strong in *challenge* believe in the value of learning from both positive and negative life events and focus on personal improvement. Those who are strong in commitment, control, *and* challenge take stressful events and turn them into chances to learn, grow, and solve a problem. The end result is that they turn problems into opportunities. These three attitudes are good predictors of how someone will deal with work and life challenges.

The Effect on Teams

In *Attitude 101*, Maxwell puts it very directly and simplistically:

- Great talent on the team + rotten attitude = Bad team
- Great talent on the team + bad attitude = Average team
- Great talent on the team + average attitude = Good team
- Great talent on the team + good attitude = Great team

Intuitively we know this is true, and any good manager works to guard the team attitude.

Success

Many writers connect success with aspects of attitude. In the October 2005 issue of *Selling*, Kelley Robertson lists several attitude related qualities that separate successful salespeople from those who are not so successful. These top performers are

- **Persistent:** They face and overcome obstacles, always have an eye out for solutions, and absolutely refuse to give up.

- **Passionate:** Usually top-performing sales professionals are thrilled about their product, organization, and daily work.

- **Enthusiastic:** They are usually in a great mood, even during times of challenge.

- **Responsible:** Performers focus on their actions and don't look to blame others. They are accountable for their actions.

- **Relational:** Top-performing sales professionals value relationships and work hard to maintain them by caring and giving.

- **Willing to give value:** Top people deliver the goods! They have an attitude of discipline when it comes to giving value to others.

Later in this book we will see how these aspects are highly connected with the attitude choices each of us can make.

The list goes on, but the main point is that attitude impacts every area of our personal life and work experience. As Ralph Waldo Emerson claimed, "If I have lost confidence in myself, I have the universe against me."

Shifting Attitude

Changing your attitude can happen over time, or it can shift very quickly. One day I was driving in my car, and a "jerk" pulled out right in front of me. Well, feeling perfectly justified I laid on my horn with the best "I am letting you know that you are a completely idiotic driver" honk my little car could muster—then I noticed something. The other driver was the elderly choir director of the church I was attending. My attitude immediately shifted from one of angry superiority to embarrassment. I was now the one at fault, not him. Then I started thinking, if this one driver wasn't really a jerk, but was rather just a good man who made a mistake, was it possible that many of those other "idiots" are also just good people who made mistakes? Of course, when I'm on the other side of the aggressive honk, I know this to be completely true! These days I try to see most drivers as human beings who make mistakes, rather than immediately summing up their entire intellect and character based on one driving event. That is a choice, and that choice shifts my attitude.

It May Not Be Easy, but It Will Be Worth It

Just because shifting your attitude is a choice does not mean it is easy to do. You do not have to look far to find someone who will try to demean your efforts to develop a top-performing attitude. We believe the appropriate response to these individuals is an appreciation for their opinion combined with a strong boundary that prevents their negativity from impacting your efforts. In truth, these individuals are simply afraid to hope for a better life. They have likely fallen prey to circumstances and events that have conditioned them to be overly protective. So gentleness and encouragement are better responses to their negativity than anger and frustration.

Have confidence that you know what you are doing and lead others to a better attitude, rather than getting dragged down and frustrated by them. Although the journey is not always easy because of this resistance, it is worth it. Albert Einstein said, "Reality is merely an illusion, albeit a very persistent one." Now some people consider him to be a pretty smart guy, so if Albert Einstein believed that you can create your own reality, maybe it's worth trying. Top performers are able to create a reality in life and work that is full of joy, opportunity, wonderful bosses, talented colleagues, and top-notch companies. As Aristotle said, "Pleasure in the job puts perfection in the work." And work is not the only thing that is touched by great attitude. People with top-performing attitudes also can create happy families and wonderful, fulfilling lives. This does not happen by accident. Many people limit their inheritance of blessings by making bad choices and giving too much power to reality. Top performers embrace the blessings of life and wisely deal with the challenges of reality.

Interviews with Top Performers

Do you dare to believe? There is power in believing—just ask sports performance psychologist Dr. Adrianne Ahern. He answered our questions about attitude by focusing on the dangers of negative thinking. Adrianne shared, "The belief that has gotten me to where I am today (and to where my top-performing athlete clients are today) is the belief that our negative thinking has simply been programmed into our heads—it does not represent the truth. In order to be free from the negativity and to create the high-performing life we see for ourselves, we have to first identify and acknowledge the negative thinking before we experience the freedom to choose the positive. Each one of us has the ability to snap out of the negativity and create expectations and visions that will take us to the top of our game, whatever our game is."

Adrianne wanted to encourage our readers to "Wake up to the possibilities that already exist within you! Trust your feelings and use your feelings to decide what type of thoughts you should entertain within your mind. When feeling joy, appreciation, love—these are indications you are on the right track!"

So again we ask, "Do you dare to believe?" If so, then get any negative thoughts out of your head and start taking your attitude to the next level by reclaiming your power. Reclaim your power by reclaiming your choice!

Putting It into Practice

Take the following informal test to determine your attitude strengths and areas where you may need improvement. Answer as honestly as possible. Note that the descriptors beneath the numbers are different for different statements.

ATTITUDE AREA 1

I frequently run into situations where I feel helpless to do anything.

-1	-2	-3	-4	-5
Rarely	Sometimes	Often	Most times	Always

I believe that I will continue to grow at a great pace for the rest of my life.

+1	+2	+3	+4	+5
Never	Rarely	Sometimes	Most times	Always

Others are responsible for my life not being what I want it to be.

-1	-2	-3	-4	-5
Rarely	Sometimes	Often	Most times	Always

I feel ashamed of myself for actions I have committed in the past.

-1	-2	-3	-4	-5
Rarely	Sometimes	Often	Most times	Always

I repeatedly talk about things that bother me.

+1	+2	+3	+4	+5
Rarely	Sometimes	Often	Most times	Always

I believe that there is a way to be successful in any situation.

+1	+2	+3	+4	+5
Never	Rarely	Sometimes	Most times	Always

I spend time strategizing about creating the future rather than focusing on the past.

+1	+2	+3	+4	+5
Never	Rarely	Sometimes	Most times	Always

ATTITUDE AREA 2

I tend to see the worst in people.

-1	-2	-3	-4	-5
Rarely	Sometimes	Often	Most times	Always

I accept other people as human and flawed and do not judge them as inferior.

+1	+2	+3	+4	+5
Never	Rarely	Sometimes	Most times	Always

I believe that it is better to protect yourself than risk being hurt by others.

-1	-2	-3	-4	-5
Rarely	Sometimes	Often	Most times	Always

When something or someone bothers me I tend to avoid having a confrontation about it.

-1	-2	-3	-4	-5
Rarely	Sometimes	Often	Most times	Always

I try to give more than I receive from others.

+1	+2	+3	+4	+5
Never	Rarely	Sometimes	Most times	Always

I find it hard to truly forgive and forget when people hurt me.

-1	-2	-3	-4	-5
Rarely	Sometimes	Often	Most times	Always

If I make a commitment to someone, I am obsessive about coming through in a timely fashion.

+1	+2	+3	+4	+5
Never	Rarely	Sometimes	Most times	Always

ATTITUDE AREA 3

I get tired of all of the change and problems this world offers.

-1	-2	-3	-4	-5
Rarely	Sometimes	Often	Most times	Always

When something goes wrong, I think it is very important to find out who is to blame.

-1	-2	-3	-4	-5
Never	Rarely	Sometimes	Most times	Always

I have a "never give up" attitude, and believe there is always a way to succeed.

+1	+2	+3	+4	+5
Rarely	Sometimes	Often	Most times	Always

I embrace and accept things I can't control.

+1	+2	+3	+4	+5
Never	Rarely	Sometimes	Most times	Always

Competition does not cause me to lose sleep; I feel there are enough rewards out there for all of us.

+1	+2	+3	+4	+5
Never	Rarely	Sometimes	Most times	Always

I think I deserve more than I am getting in life.

-1	-2	-3	-4	-5
Rarely	Sometimes	Often	Most times	Always

I focus on my own areas of life and business and ignore those of the whole community.

-1	-2	-3	-4	-5
Rarely	Sometimes	Often	Most times	Always

ANSWERS

Attitude Area #1

For attitude area #1, add up all of the numbers that have a "+" in front of them and put the total here: _____.

For attitude area #1, add up all of the numbers that have a "–" in front of them and put the total here: _____.

Subtract the negative numbers from the positive numbers and put the result here:

Attitude area #1 total: _____

Attitude Area #2

For attitude area #2, add up all of the numbers that have a "+" in front of them and put the total here: _____.

For attitude area #2, add up all of the numbers that have a "−" in front of them and put the total here: _____.

Subtract the negative numbers from the positive numbers and put the result here:

Attitude area #2 total: _____

Attitude Area #3

For attitude area #3, add up all of the numbers that have a "+" in front of them and put the total here: _____.

For attitude area #3, add up all of the numbers that have a "−" in front of them and put the total here: _____.

Subtract the negative numbers from the positive numbers and put the result here:

THE TOP PERFORMER'S GUIDE TO ATTITUDE

Attitude area #3 total: _____

What Does It All Mean?

Self: Attitude Area #1 represents how you see yourself. It reveals your view of your personal power. We will cover your personal attitude choices in Chapter 3.

Others: Attitude Area #2 reflects those beliefs, feelings, and actions that form your attitudes about other people, which will be addressed in Chapter 4.

The world: Attitude Area #3 represents your choices about how you view and interact with the world, which we will explore in Chapter 5.

Together, these three attitude areas demonstrate how closely your attitude resembles that of a top performer. The following are guidelines to suggest how you should view your scores in each area.

- **10 to 11:** Wow! You could have written this book—you have the attitude of a top performer. Use this book to reinforce your great attitude and encourage friends!

- **6 to 9:** Congratulations, you have a better attitude than most people, and with a little tweaking, you will have a top-performing attitude.

- **–5 to 5:** Don't despair; your attitude is like those of most people. However, we know you don't want to be average, so use this book to go to the next level.

- **–11 to –6:** Okay, we have some work to do, but with dedication and effort you can kick that attitude up a notch or two (or maybe all the way).

- **–12 to –17:** You may be going through a particularly tough time right now or have a longer-term struggle with attitude. Try to fight the skepticism that you will feel working through this book and truly use this as a chance to transform.

If one particular area is low—for example, you may have good scores in area #1 but struggle with area #2—make sure you focus on the chapter that represents that area.

SECTION II

ATTITUDE
CHOICES

CHAPTER 2

HOW YOU SEE AND TREAT YOURSELF: SEVEN CHOICES ABOUT YOUR PERSONAL POWER

Attitude Adages

To put the world right in order, we must first put the nation in order; to put the nation in order, we must first put the family in order; to put the family in order, we must first cultivate our personal life; we must first set our hearts right.

—Confucius

What counts is not necessarily the size of the dog in the fight— it's the size of the fight in the dog.

—Dwight Eisenhower

In a Nutshell

The first set of top-performing attitude choices concerns each of us individually. What do you really believe about your power to impact your life and workplace? What do you truly think about taking chances to shine? Do you take risks, or do you play your cards cautiously? Our beliefs about our identity, power, and abilities will dictate our success. These beliefs have the power to lead us to lives of shame, apathy, and despair or to help us live with confidence and passion. In this chapter we examine seven choices you can make concerning who you are and what you are able to do.

It's All in How You Look at It

One of my favorite movies is *The Shawshank Redemption*. In this movie, a man named Andy has been falsely imprisoned and spends years slowly digging his way out of prison with a tiny rock hammer. While in prison he experiences many abuses, disappointments, and setbacks. In a particularly emotional sequence, Andy is having a debate with a fellow prisoner named Red. Andy had just gotten out of solitary confinement for going against the authorities and playing classical music over the prison loudspeakers. Their conversation goes like this:

> Andy: *That's the beauty of music. They can't get that from you. . . . Haven't you ever felt that way about music?*
>
> Red: *I played a mean harmonica as a younger man. Lost interest in it though. Didn't make much sense in here.*
>
> Andy: *Here's where it makes the most sense. You need it so you don't forget.*
>
> Red: *Forget?*
>
> Andy: *Forget that . . . there are places in this world that aren't made out of stone. That there's something inside . . . that they can't get to, that they can't touch. That's yours.*

Red: What're you talking about?
Andy: Hope.

Andy knew that hope has power. And with hope and tenacity, he finally gains his freedom in a scene that would have the most cynical person jumping out of his chair and cheering. His journey represents the first choice you have to make about your personal power.

Hopeful vs. Helpless

Choosing helplessness ensures poor performance, lackluster morale, and low confidence. Voltaire said, "I am a little deaf, a little blind, a little impotent, and on top of this are two or three abominable infirmities, but nothing destroys my hope." Voltaire knew that even in the darkest times we must hold out hope. Without hope we have despair. Many talented individuals who go through tough times subconsciously choose helplessness over hope and never live to the fullest of their abilities.

Hope simply means that you trust and expect that good things will happen. By expecting good things, you invite them into your life and are more likely to receive them. Hope does *not* mean that you ignore the reality of difficult times, but rather that you look for opportunity during them. The author of *Think and Grow Rich* and one of the greatest motivators of the last century, Napoleon Hill, said, "Opportunity . . . often it comes in the form of misfortune, or temporary defeat." Hope is simply the belief that if you try long and hard enough, something good will come from it. Even if you don't get your perfect desired outcome, at least you will grow from the struggle!

The choice to be hopeful has incredible power to create your future. The choice to believe that you are helpless will guarantee that you are indeed. The habit of believing in your powerlessness has an insidious impact. In the words of Tyron Edwards, "Any act often repeated soon forms a habit; and habit allowed, steadily gains in strength. At first it may be but as the spider's web, easily broken through, but if not resisted it soon binds us with chains of steel." Hopelessness is just like that spider's web. Once we are trapped in that belief, it is nearly impossible to break out.

Now you may be thinking, "You just don't know the stuff that I have been through—it is different." Well, you are right that we do not know you and all of the details of your struggle, and if we could hear the details we would probably empathize with you. What we do know is that most top performers attribute their abilities to the fact that they have gone through difficult times. Whether it is a company merger, a job loss, a tough boss, or any other challenging factor you face, hope can help you learn and grow. The first choice you need to make in hope versus helpless is your decision to believe that your attitude is within your power. You must believe that you can take charge of your attitude.

Potential vs. Stagnation

We recently started a sales-skills workshop by asking the participants what would make the workshop worthwhile for them. We asked, "What challenges do you face in your job?" and "If you could get anything from our time together, what would you like to get?" Most participants made insightful comments, but one gentleman boldly exclaimed that he had mastered his job. There was nothing for him to learn, and our workshop was going to be a waste of time (he said this not even knowing the content of the workshop, of course). For most of the workshop he did not participate, and at times we had to confront him for disruptive behavior. We found out from his boss that this gentleman was decent at his job. The manager went on to say that the gentleman was good, but he was not—and if he keeps the same attitude will never be—great. He had chosen stagnation over potential. He had chosen good over great.

In the book *Good to Great*, Jim Collins shares how *good* can often be the greatest detriment to someone becoming *great*. Although we are not saying that "good enough" is bad, what we are claiming is that it does not fit the attitude of a top performer. People like Tiger Woods and Lance Armstrong never take the stance of "I can't get any better," despite the fact that they are clearly masters of their sports. They continue to tweak and hone their abilities. They are constantly looking to improve. To them, stagnation is unacceptable—they continually strive to be better. Benjamin Franklin said, "Be always at war with your vices, at peace with your neighbors, and let each new year find you a better man." (It should go without saying that this, like all of our quotes, fully applies to both men and women.)

Pride gives us a temporary sense of superiority. We feel impressive because, unlike the rest of the slobs in the room, we don't need to change a thing about ourselves. We take the Popeye defense: "I yam what I yam." Unfortunately, as the proverb says, "Pride goeth before the fall." Prideful people usually feel pain later on in life when they discover that they have remained stagnant while others around them have grown. This often destroys careers and even relationships. It takes humility and confidence to pursue growth. Take Baltimore Orioles shortstop Miguel Tejada, who arrived at spring training camp in 2007 vowing to be "a different Miguel." This vow came the year after he was named Most Valuable Oriole for the second time in three seasons, led the team with a .300 average, 24 home runs, 100 RBIs, and set a club record with 214 hits. Stagnated players may have taken refuge in the perception of being valued, but Tejada started his season with a proclamation of change for the better. Top performers care less about comparing themselves to others and more about comparing themselves to what they could be. And their vision of what they could be is usually a big vision.

Ownership vs. Victimhood

This next choice area has the greatest chance for misinterpretation; it is the choice between ownership and victimhood. It is important that we point out the difference between adopting the *identity* of a victim and simply accepting the fact that you were victimized. In life we can experience terrible hurts, and this section is absolutely *not* about taking responsibility off of a perpetrator's shoulders. That responsibility stays there. This is about maintaining an identity of empowerment even when someone has hurt you.

Back when I was a therapist, I allowed people to stay in a victim mode longer than what was probably best for them. Although I continue to believe that it is critical for someone to vent and process how others' actions have hurt them, I also believe that if we encourage someone to keep recycling hurtful memories, we cause major damage to their identity. And telling a person, "It wasn't your fault" is certainly kind on the surface, but it also completely erases any power that the person had in the situation, and will have over future situations. It means that they are helpless to prevent themselves from being victimized again.

Whether you were hurt by a parent, a spouse, peers, or a boss, you have the power to eventually get yourself out of that situation and heal. This doesn't mean that it is your fault that they hurt you, but it means that *only* you have the power to choose to let that hurt continue or to put an end to it for good. You have the power to stand up to them and leave, or you can meekly accept the situation. It is your choice. If you believe that you are a victim, then you will act like a victim. And what do victims do? They get victimized! However, if you are a strong, capable person who unfortunately got hurt by someone, you certainly can learn from that experience and not allow it to happen to you again. You have power! Best-selling author Carlos Castaneda captured it well when he said, "A warrior takes responsibility for his acts, for the most trivial of acts. An average man acts out his thoughts, and never takes responsibility for what he does." Top performers do not see themselves as victims. Even if hurt or attacked, they never take the identity of a victim. They know full well the rewards that come with 100% ownership.

Victor Frankl addressed this in his writings about his experiences as a prisoner in the Nazi prison camps. He stated, "We who lived in concentration camps can remember the men who walked through the huts comforting others, giving away their last piece of bread. They may have been few in number, but they offer sufficient proof that everything can be taken from a man but one thing; the last of the human freedoms—to choose one's attitude in any given set of circumstances, to choose one's own way." In this situation, individuals were horribly victimized, but some did not allow themselves to become victims. They stayed focused on what they could control, their attitude.

Most of us will never experience this level of victimization, but we are presented with subtle choices every day that can lead us to adopt the victim identity. If you find yourself constantly complaining about your coworkers, your employees, or your boss, you are most likely stuck in this mode. You don't have to be a victim. For example, we have seen employees grumble about assignments they have been given and how overloaded they are, and yet they refuse to say no to anything for fear of disappointing a boss, coworker, or some other person of consequence. Who needs to take responsibility for that? It is not your boss's job to say no for you. A top performer asks for help prioritizing tasks given by their boss and has the ability to negotiate tasks and duties in a positive and cooperative manner. When we choose to take responsibility for the pressure we put on ourselves to please others, we own our emotions, our work, and our life. As Nobel Peace Prize winner Dag Hammarskjold put it, "Is life so wretched? Isn't it rather your hands which are too small, your vision which is muddled? You are the one who must grow up."

Conviction vs. Shame

We have just addressed when someone has done something wrong to you, but how do top performers handle it when they have failed to achieve the outcome they were striving for? What if you mess up on a key account and you have to tell your boss? How would you feel?

"Shame on you" is a phrase that many of us heard growing up. But what do top performers do with shame? Do they even believe in it? First, let's look at the difference between guilt, shame, and conviction. Here is how we view these:

- Guilt = "I've done something wrong."
- Shame = "I am something wrong."
- Conviction = "I will do better."

People with top-performing attitudes are not immune to making mistakes; however, they do not dwell on the mistake or let the mistake impact their identity. When our flaws impact our identities, we start believing that we are more defective than the rest of the population—we feel shame. Now although it is true that we all have defects, it is also true that being flawed is part of being human, and we all need to work on our flaws rather than be consumed by them. We have also worked intimately with enough people to know that *no one* has it all together. No one! We each have our flaws and our gifts.

Shame does not serve us, because it is self-focused and drains us of ambition and drive.

Conviction, on the other hand, is a powerful emotion that helps move us further ahead in life. Conviction (along with attitudes such as passion, fervor, and assurance) focuses on creating the future rather than dwelling in the past. In many ways shame is selfish. I remember a time in my life when I had done something reprehensible, and shame was trying to grip me in its deadly hands. A friend helped me greatly by asking me how my shame was serving the world. He challenged me to quit thinking about myself and to think more about serving others. I realized that I could choose to either feel shame and sink into a deep depression or admit my mistakes and focus on making things better for anyone who would allow me to make amends. I really believe that I would still be stuck in the quagmire of selfish depression if I had chosen shame. Shame serves no one. Of course, neither does the person who denies wrongdoing and simply blames others.

Individuals who face their mistakes, own them, and decide to do differently are often the most passionate at championing positive causes and changing the world. Shame creates self-centered thoughts—Bad *me!* Woe is *me! I'm* terrible!—while conviction is selfless: What do *my coworkers* need from me? How can I make it up to *the company?* What do I need to do to make amends to *others?*

Top performers have an attitude of conviction, and conviction is the emotional fuel for creating something better than what they created in the past.

Venting vs. Whining

Shame has a relative called self-pity. Author John Garner said, "Self-pity is easily the most destructive of the nonpharmaceutical narcotics; it is addictive, gives momentary pleasure, and separates the victim from reality." Have you ever fallen to the temptation of self-pity? Self-pity usually shows up as whining. Think about any coworkers who constantly complain about their boss, the hours they work, or the pay they make. After a while you don't even want to be around them because you could repeat their complaints verbatim. But don't psychologists tell us that venting emotion is a good thing? The key is to discover the difference between whining and venting. We see it this way: Venting is whining with a purpose.

When you vent, you have a reason for talking about the issue. You want to release it and free yourself from the captivity that would surely come with self-pity. In contrast, someone who is whining simply recycles the pain. They want to make sure that everyone knows their burdens. They want a spotlight on the pain rather than a spot remover.

Want to vent? Great! Write a letter to the person with whom you are angry and blast them to smithereens. Then rip up the letter, go to them, and calmly deal with the issue. Hit a punching bag or go jogging and think to yourself, "I am releasing this hurt," rather than sitting on the couch with a vodka tonic and imagining all the hurt that people have dealt you in your life. If the boss is pressuring you and you feel it is too much to handle, go talk to her instead of running to your colleagues and being conspirators in attacking her character flaws and lack of leadership. What does that solve? Whining serves no one, especially you! It is a temporary fix to a far bigger issue. Top performers know that sometimes they need to vent and release the poison from their bodies. But they do this in a productive and effective way, and then they go deal with the situation.

Dream vs. Doubt

In his famous speech, Dr. Martin Luther King, Jr. proclaimed, "I have a dream." Imagine if this speech, which has captivated us for decades, went like this: "I have a dream. Now I'm not sure this will really happen. In fact, there are so many things that could mess it up that I don't want anyone getting their hopes up . . ." Not real inspiring, is it?

Dr. Norman Vincent Peale (author of *The Power of Positive Thinking*) said, "Become a possibilitarian. No matter how dark things seem to be or actually are, raise your sights and see possibilities—always see them for they're always there." When you find yourself in an ambiguous situation, do you dream or do you doubt? Are you optimistic or pessimistic? The optimist sees the possibilities and believes there is a way to eventually get a positive result from any situation. The pessimist sees only the black hole of obstacles and doubts a positive outcome. While top performers see the same challenges that pessimists do, top performers believe them to be mere stepping stones on their path to a positive outcome. Their motto is "There is always a way." This does not mean that they believe that they will always get exactly what they want. Rather, they just dream of the positive things that will eventually come with tenacity and wise actions. They are optimistic in their ability to create a positive future. As author James Allen said, "The dreamers are the saviors of the world."

Thomas Jefferson said, "Doubts . . . often beget the facts they fear." Doubts create fear and hesitation and sap your energy. Dreams create courage, boldness, and tenacity. Dreamers also create an unstoppable joy in living. An Italian proverb captures this well: "Since the house is on fire let us warm ourselves." There is good to be found in almost any situation, and an attitude of optimism will help increase your chances of a dream coming true. On one level it is common sense to choose dreaming over doubting. As Winston Churchill claimed, "I am an optimist. It does not seem too much use being anything else." Top performers know that being a pessimist simply does not serve us. There are merits in recognizing challenges, but allowing obstacles to overwhelm us does not make our lives better in any way. The ability to imagine a great future is crucial to your success. Albert Einstein stated, "Your imagination is your preview to life's coming attractions." Oh, doubters may preach to dreamers that what they are trying to do is impossible, but as Walt Disney boldly proclaimed, "It's kind of fun to do the impossible."

Past vs. Future

One winter day I was passing another car on the Illinois tollway and glanced in my rear view mirror only to see a car barreling up behind me in the snow. As quickly as safety would allow, I got over in the right lane and watched him go speeding past. Later I saw the same car in a ditch with another car that it must have hit. Had I not used my rearview mirror, it might have been me in that ditch. Another day, I was driving down the highway and saw a car in front of me driving erratically. As I went to pass, I saw a woman talking on her cell phone with one hand while staring in the rearview mirror and applying mascara with her other hand (she must have been driving with her knee). I quickly got away from this dangerous driver. She was an accident waiting to happen.

Cars have rearview mirrors for a reason. It is good to check your rearview mirror as you drive, because it can alert you to dangers that are behind you. However, only the most foolish of drivers stays completely focused on the rearview mirror. Their attention must be primarily focused on the road ahead, or they are vulnerable to an accident. The same thing is true for our lives. In life, the rearview mirror represents the past. It is good to look at, know, and accept what has occurred to us in the past. However, it is not helpful to keep our full attention on the past. Our eyes must mainly gaze toward the future. Top performers envision a great future. They feel empowered to create a future that is successful and fulfilling. Those stuck staring into their rearview mirror carry around the hurts from a former boss, colleague, employee, or significant other. They live in fear of experiencing the past again and hamper their risk-taking and creativity because of this fear. The top performer can experience a lay-off, a bad boss, an unethical company, or anything else unsavory or hurtful, and leave it in the past. Napoleon Hill once wrote, "Before success comes in any man's life he is sure to meet with much temporary defeat and, perhaps, some failures. When defeat overtakes a man, the easiest and most logical thing to do is to quit. That is exactly what the majority of men do." Defeat will only overtake you if you give the past power. Choose to embrace your past, but focus on creating a better future.

Interviews with Top Performers

Drew Stevens, PhD, is an author and sales expert. When asked what viewpoint had gotten him where he is today, he said that his main belief was "To move forward and not be afraid to fail. Failure is God's greatest tutor. Top performers take risks and sometimes things go wrong, yet risk keeps you moving forward." Drew knows that risk is essential in order to grow and to thrive. He added, "Attitude is latitude, if you remain positive, all things around you are positive. Keep a positive attitude, smile often, visualize success, and you will achieve more than you think possible."

Putting It into Practice

Fill in the chart below to gain insight into the choices you are making daily concerning your personal power.

Attitudes about yourself	What are some warning signs that you are falling into the negative choice?	What corrective actions can you do at those moments that will help you make the positive choice?
Hopeful vs. Helpless		
Potential vs. Stagnation		
Ownership vs. Victimhood		
Conviction vs. Shame		
Venting vs. Whining		
Dream vs. Doubt		
Past vs. Future		

CHAPTER 3

HOW YOU VIEW AND INTERACT WITH OTHERS: SEVEN CHOICES ABOUT YOUR COWORKERS

Attitude Adages

Doubt yourself and you doubt everything you see. Judge yourself and you see judges everywhere. But if you listen to the sound of your own voice, you can rise above doubt and judgment. And you can see forever.

—Olympic Figure-Skating Medalist Nancy Kerrigan

There are two types of people—those who come into a room and say, "Well, here I am!" and those who come in and say, "Ah, there you are."

—Author Frederick L. Collins

In a Nutshell

Whether you are a Fortune 500 executive or a stay-at-home parent, your workplace can either fill your life with joy or with frustration. It can be difficult to maintain a positive attitude when we have to deal with people who have strong differences from our own, people of different abilities, and those who have not developed a strong sense of teamwork and collaboration. Our assumptions and judgments will impact how we treat our coworkers and, in return, how we are treated (which, in turn, will impact performance). In this chapter we examine seven choices you can make concerning your beliefs, emotions, and behaviors related to those around you.

It's All in How You Look at It

In Dr. David Niven's *The 100 Simple Secrets of Happy People*, we find evidence for how attitude in relationships is related to our life happiness. He discusses the following research findings:

- Glass and Jolly (1997) discovered that having a positive view of those around us is one of the most powerful predictors of our happiness.
- Sugarman (1997) found that happiness is increased almost 30 percent by community involvement.
- Turner (1994) showed that happiness is not related to the number of conflicts we have, but rather to the follow-up to commitments arising from the conflict.
- Williams, Haber, Weaver, and Freeman (1998) suggested that altruism increases life satisfaction by 24 percent.

Attitude is highly dependent on your satisfaction with your relationships, and in this chapter we will examine how your choices about your coworkers, family, and others shape your attitude. The first two choices are related and address how you view other human beings.

Strengths vs. Flaws

If you have picked up any of our previous books, you know we are very focused on how people deal with the normal differences between one another. For example, I was once traveling with a friend, and we pulled into a gas station for a fill up. The station had multiple pumps, and it was very busy this particular morning. After dodging a few cars we finally got to our pump. My friend got out of the car, unscrewed the gas cap, grabbed the nozzle off the pump and then, looking around, hesitated. After about ten seconds of deliberation, without putting any gas in the car, he put the nozzle back on the pump, screwed the cap back on the tank, and got back in the car. He then proceeded to drive around the multiple cars at the pumps, weaving in and out until he arrived back at the same pump we were at previously, except pointed in the opposite direction. To understand my confusion, you have to know that the tank was under the license plate, so the direction of the vehicle should not have mattered in the slightest. After he got out, unscrewed the gas cap, grabbed the nozzle, and filled up the tank he returned to the car. He responded to my mystified look with, "Oh, there was a slight incline in the pavement and I was able to get more gas in by pointing the car in the opposite direction." Seeing my struggle to wrap my head around this concept he added, "It's just the way I like to do things."

To me, that was not an efficient way to get gas, and I began noticing other perfectionistic patterns with my friend. I had a choice—do I see my friend as flawed, or do I see the strengths he brings with his perspectives? If I focus on his flaws, then I will ruminate about the inefficiencies, rigidity, and, well, weird behaviors. If I focus on strengths, then I will see his uncanny ability to adjust to the smallest details and perfect something way beyond my capabilities. Don't get me wrong; I don't want to be like him. This is not about believing his path or behavior is better than mine. This is about seeing his positive side instead of focusing on what I don't like. The amount of time you spend around traits you perceive as flaws impacts your happiness and productivity—so, what if you decide *not* to see these traits as flaws? Top performers see and celebrate the unique strengths in their coworkers and leverage those differences to create a successful team. As psychiatrist Carl Jung said, "Everything that irritates us about others can lead us to an understanding of ourselves."

Accepting vs. Judging

Our previous section dealt with focusing on other's behaviors; this section examines your judgment of the whole person. How do you view others when they do something negative? We believe that Americans love reality television because we love to celebrate other people's flaws. Judging them feeds our temporary sense of self-worth with a false sense of superiority. Of course, judging others is different than judging behavior. Most of us have a moral code that we (sometimes inconsistently) follow. This code is formed through experience, modeling from key influences, teachings, religion, and other factors; and we will always have natural judgments about behavior. That fits the attitude of a top performer—they have strong opinions about work ethic, treatment of coworkers, project management, and so forth. However, when judgment moves from assessing behavior to the labeling and dismissal of a person, nothing good follows.

For example, take an individual who has a strong entrepreneurial spirit and works in a hierarchical work culture. This person is often off doing their own thing, doesn't ask permission before making and initiating key decisions, and many times shows a strong desire not to be managed by another person. Is this individual a bad worker, jerk, or rebel? Or may there just be a poor fit between this individual's strengths and the culture of this particular company? Top performers tend to focus on finding a good fit for a person, rather than labeling them inadequate. They have an attitude that allows for differences in the workplace and can also determine when someone is a square peg in a round hole. Instead of complaining about this and assassinating the character of the worker, they have discussions of fit and look to match the right person to the right job. They accept the person, rather than judge them.

Judging others rarely leads to a good attitude or a good outcome. The Christian Bible is full of verses such as "Judge not, lest you be judged." Yet as a pastor's son, I can tell you that many Christians (as well as people from other religions that share this philosophy) fail miserably to carry this out in its entirety. Others go too far and claim that there is no right or wrong, rendering a decision impossible. The top performer balances these out. He or she will judge some behaviors in order to keep an organization running at peak performance. However, they accept that organizations are made up of talented people who are different and even flawed. They have an attitude that allows others to mold their strengths in a safe environment, or move on to the environment that matches their drives and abilities (without sending them away with a message of failure). A mind filled with judgment is a mind filled with negativity. And a mind filled with negativity does not create the attitude of a top performer.

Open vs. Closed

I remember taking a road trip with a friend who decided to share all the ins and outs of his sex life. For forty-five minutes we discussed what he was happy about, unhappy about, and apathetic about. After finishing up this discussion, we started discussing his career. He opened with, "I just am not happy with the amount of money I make." To which I asked, "How much do you make?" He curtly responded with, "That's personal."

I find it very interesting what topics we are open about and what topics we keep close to the vest. My friend was extremely open about his sex life (something many would not be open about) and yet shut down completely when we had a discussion about money. Now, we are not saying that you need to talk at work about either how much you make or how much you, well . . . you know. Rather we just want to discuss the role of self-protection and how it will impact your attitude toward others and their attitude toward you.

I am often called upon to coach workers who are known as being overly aggressive. However, once I get to know them, they usually turn out to be nice people. Eventually I discover that they are hiding that side of themselves from their coworkers. They are afraid of being hurt, so they refuse to be vulnerable. In turn, their peers see them as standoffish, cold, or controlling, and so they respond negatively. Both parties are contributing to the negative attitude and are building more and more bad feelings in the office. Part of my job is to help my clients see that their closed presence contributes to the negativity they are receiving from others. Although they fear being more open and vulnerable, often it is the only way to overcome the false image they have projected.

There are many reasons why you may have chosen to close off from others. People are imperfect and will hurt you at times. You may have had a previous bad experience and are fearful of going through the same thing again. That is all completely understandable. However, just because something is understandable does not necessarily mean that it's the best attitude choice. Unless you are working in a truly dangerous and psychologically dysfunctional setting, the combination of strength and vulnerability often invites understanding and reciprocal vulnerability. Self-protection only invites judgment and abandonment.

Individuals with a strong need to protect their ego will often have to sacrifice honesty in some situations to protect their ego. This makes you feel like an imposter and, worse, leaves you feeling like a hamster running on a wheel, constantly in motion due to your fear of someone catching onto the real you. For example, I was with a group of rookie business coaches years ago, and they started a conversation about fees. One of the coaches proudly stated, "I charge $500 per hour for my coaching." I watched as all of the other coaches' eyes got big, and they started asking tons of questions to understand how he could charge that much. As the conversation continued I noticed the "expensive" coach hemming and hawing some, and I decided to ask him how many clients he had at $500 an hour. With a little confrontation and detailed questioning, we finally got his answer: none.

When we close ourselves off and try to protect our ego, we often lose our integrity—and once your integrity is gone, your attitude is hollow. Top performers are open about both their flaws and their abilities. They do not get trapped by pride and instead accept who they are and who they are becoming. They are playing to win in life and take risks, instead of playing not to lose—falling into conservative thinking and self-protection.

Confronting vs. Avoiding

There are few things more dangerous to a top-performing attitude than the avoidance of problems. I explore this tendency in great detail in the book *The Coward's Guide to Conflict*, but here we will touch on it briefly. Although we empathize with people who avoid conflict, we also know the dangers that come from chronically avoiding things that need confrontation. When we avoid we simply:

- Recycle the pain (because it keeps reoccurring due to the lack of solution).
- Decrease our confidence.
- Reinforce fear.

A simple example is to consider your work day. Think about that one activity or discussion that you dread doing. Do you put it off, or do you do it right away? When you put it off, you are likely thinking about it several times during your day (you re-experience the dread/pain each time). You also are impacting your confidence, because on some level you doubt your ability to handle the issue. Also, you are living in fear (or at least a state of internal tension), which is not good for anything, including your long-term health. We do better when we take the advice of author Nicholas Chamfort, who said, "Swallow a toad in the morning and you will encounter nothing more disgusting the rest of the day." Failing to tackle dreaded activities impacts your attitude for the entire day. It drains your energy and your concentration. Orison Swett Marden captured it well with, "Most of our obstacles would melt away if, instead of cowering before them, we should make up our minds to walk boldly through them."

Do you walk boldly, or do you cower? Top performers are willing to go through the discomfort of confronting because they know the impact it has on their confidence and well-being. Although they may not look forward to the confrontation, they envision positive outcomes and make their best attempt to positively effect the situation.

Giving vs. Taking

One thing we have noticed about every true top performer is that they give more than they take. They freely share their success tactics, information, and powerful processes with coworkers and do not seem to fear that they will lose out because of this behavior. In some ways this is counter-intuitive. Shouldn't we be happier the more we take (i.e., get)? So we have to go a little deeper than the obvious to understand this phenomenon.

First of all, top performers take great joy in impacting others. It is an intrinsic joy that can only be found in someone who celebrates doing something just because it is the right thing to do. Now, we are not referring to the person who reluctantly gives to others—that person is usually not joyful and is giving only out of feelings of obligation or guilt. Top performers are not driven primarily by negative emotions, and they create the life they want by contributing to the lives of others.

Second, top performers give because they know that giving without expectation of equal compensation actually creates more compensation. When we expect people to give back to us, we are inviting obligatory giving. This rarely creates an attitude of joy and selflessness. The top performer gives without expecting equality. There is no balance sheet. By giving with an attitude of selflessness, the top performer creates a community of people who have each others' backs, so to speak.

Taking creates a temporary treasure that may give brief glimpses of impermanent happiness. But takers eventually wear out their welcome and eventually create a community that withdraws from them. In addition, research from Dr. Martin Seligman finds that acts of altruism actually build confidence and self-esteem. So the next time you are struggling with your attitude, go out and do something kind for someone else. Give to someone and you will receive, at the very minimum, a better attitude. One of our favorite passages in the Christian New Testament is Jesus interacting with the disciples as they ask him about the greatest commandment. His reply captures the heart of the giver: "You shall love the Lord your God with all your heart, and with all your soul, and with all your mind. This is the great and first commandment. And the second is like it, you shall love your neighbor as yourself." Although this kind of language may seem strong for the workplace, we would challenge you to bring an attitude of love to all around you and just see what that creates. Share what you know and build a top-performing team of individuals who do the same.

Forgiving vs. Holding

In the previous chapter we looked at how to view yourself when you have been hurt by someone else. Now we want to explore how to view and relate to others when you are truly harmed by someone's selfishness or evil intention. What kind of attitude do top performers take in that type of situation? From working with hundreds of top performers over the years, we can tell you that very few of them waste time on replaying the harms that people have done them in the past. They do not hold on to the sins people have committed against them. They forgive instead of hold. They know, as Confucius knew, "To be wronged is nothing unless you continue to remember it."

There have been times that we have been coaching people on teams who are holding grudges against other team members. As we bring up the topic of forgiveness, they often say something along the lines of "They don't deserve to be forgiven." In this statement lies the paradox of forgiveness. If someone deserves forgiveness, then it is not forgiveness they need. Forgiveness can only be given when someone does *not* deserve it. Otherwise you are simply offering them fairness. When you choose to hold on to hurts from others, your attitude is contaminated by bitterness. It is difficult to live a life of optimism and joy when you hold someone hostage to your lack of forgiveness. Country singer Tim McGraw has a wonderful song called "Live Like You Were Dying." In the song he wisely shares the number of activities one might do if he knew that he was going to die. Along with going sky-diving and loving better he shares, "I gave forgiveness I'd been denying." Giving forgiveness to others is a freeing activity. By releasing your bitterness toward them, you free yourself up from being a hostage to their crime.

Some worry about the concept of forgiveness because they feel it will make them vulnerable to being hurt again, and there is some validity in that. However, it is possible to forgive and at the same time have strong boundaries. For example, if a coworker steals your work and presents it as his, it is normal to feel cautious about sharing work in the future. You can forgive as well as put very clear boundaries on how your work is to be shared. Some of this has to do with your understanding of what forgiveness truly is. In a definition of forgiveness that could only be generated by scientists, Thompson and Snyder define it as the "framing of a perceived transgression such that one's attachment to the transgressor, transgression, and sequelae of the transgression is transformed from negative to neutral or positive." In common language, they're saying that forgiveness just means that your emotions toward someone are no longer negative. It does not mean that they are your best friend or most trusted colleague, but it does mean that you are not consumed with negativity in their presence. Top performers know that forgiveness is good for your soul and for your attitude. Teams who hold on to wrongs are not truly teams. They need to confront the issues, work out solutions, and then focus on the future.

Delivering vs. Disappointing

This particular attitude choice reveals the difference between people with great attitudes and those who pretend to be positive and convicted but are really all talk. These individuals will promise you the world, but are not willing to put in the hard work necessary to make it happen. Top performers have more than a "can do" attitude—they have a "will do" attitude. If they tell you it will be done, it will be done. They deliver rather than disappoint. As legendary coach Vince Lombardi puts it, "If you aren't fired with enthusiasm, you will be fired with enthusiasm." Top performers match their enthusiasm with their actions.

Have you ever been in a relationship with someone who frequently overpromises and underdelivers? It is extremely frustrating to be disappointed by someone's false promises. As scholar Joel Barker puts it, "Vision without action is merely a dream. Action without vision just passes the time. Vision with action can change the world." When you deliver what you promise, you convey an attitude of confidence and integrity instead of simply looking good on the surface and then having to constantly make excuses to the people you disappoint.

Top performers know that a genuinely powerful attitude is 100 percent connected to action. In fact, some may argue that your actions will reveal far more about your attitude than anything you say. To borrow an overused phrase, those that talk the talk but do not walk the walk have given the positive attitude a bad reputation. People will always believe what you *do* rather than what you *say*. If you are a top performer, you will work like no one else will to deliver on your promises. Top performers know that great results and opportunities come with sweat and effort. As Thomas Jefferson once said, "I'm a great believer in luck and I find the harder I work, the more I have of it." And as Thomas Edison said, "Opportunity is missed by most because it is dressed in overalls and looks like work."

Interviews with Top Performers

Carole Cowperthwaite-O'Hagan is an executive coach and trainer with Advantage Coaching & Training and the CEO of CAE, Inc. She is also a good friend. To understand Carole and her attitude, you would have needed to see her on her fortieth birthday. We were in San Diego, California, and had completed a keynote address earlier that day. We decided to celebrate her birthday by going dancing. It was 9:00 p.m., and no one was on the dance floor, but that did not stop Carole. She went out immediately and started dancing. For some, that alone would take a very confident attitude. However, the real magic of the evening was to watch Carole's infectious attitude on others. The only time she came off the dance floor was to grab some strangers by the arm (usually a couple, so she was grabbing two arms) and encourage these shy strangers to get out on the floor and boogie! At first the crowd thought she was a bit odd and most resisted her invitations to come out of their shell, but soon they changed their view and were rocking to sounds of the '80s. When we finally dragged Carole off of the dance floor (since we had to present the next day again), the people who had been strangers fought our attempts to remove her. They had found a new friend, someone who brought them out of their shyness and helped them have a wonderful evening. They were drawn to Carole and did not want her to leave. That is the attitude Carole brings to everything she does. Coach Carole had the following to say about attitude.

There are beliefs I have formed over time that I believe are crucial to living life well. They are:

- You need to believe in yourself first before you can expect anyone else to believe in you.
- Fill your mind with positive thoughts and words, especially when someone may say something negative to you or about you.
- Good things happen to good people as long as you believe.
- Give more than you take.
- Never compromise your values or lose yourself. You are great just the way you are.

Carole knows the incredible impact you can bring to others by sharing your attitude freely and generously.

Putting It into Practice

Fill in the chart below to gain insight into the choices you are making daily about others.

Attitudes about others	What are some warning signs that you are falling into the negative choice?	What corrective actions can you do at those moments that will help you make the positive choice?
Strengths vs. Flaws		
Accepting vs. Judging		
Open vs. Closed		
Confronting vs. Avoiding		
Giving vs. Taking		
Forgiving vs. Holding		
Delivering vs. Disappointing		

CHAPTER 4

HOW YOU PERCEIVE AND RELATE TO THE WORLD: SEVEN CHOICES RELATED TO YOUR WORK

Attitude Adages

Could we change our attitude, we should not only see life differently, but life itself would come to be different.

—Short-Story Writer Katherine Mansfield

A loving person lives in a loving world. A hostile person lives in a hostile world; everyone you meet is your mirror.

—Author Ken Keyes, Jr.

In a Nutshell

In this chapter, take your efforts up another notch and look at how you relate to the world (and, therefore, how you view your workplace). This chapter addresses your relationship with things that you can't control. Do you deal with these things like a top performer? Within this chapter you will find the secrets that make top performers succeed in environments that give them limited control. We will look at seven choices you can make concerning your view of those things in life that are bigger than you. We will also explore how *deserve* can be a very dangerous word and why tenacity is so core to the top performer.

It's All in How You Look at It

In Dr. David Niven's *The 100 Simple Secrets of Happy People*, we find evidence for how attitude in relationships is related to our life happiness. He discusses the following research findings: Bethany Hamilton was featured on CNN's Web site on November 25, 2003, in an article called "Teen shark victim: Can't wait to surf again." Bethany was 13 when she lost her left arm to a shark attack while surfing. The article stated, "[Bethany] said her family and faith helped her to maintain a positive attitude throughout the ordeal." So what is the result of Bethany's positive attitude? Well, this young woman has appeared on *Oprah*, is pursued for speaking engagements, has written several books, is the focus of a documentary, and even has a cosmetic line. Oh, and more importantly, she still surfs and loves it! She has won or placed well in many national contests despite her so-called handicap. Because of Bethany's attitude, an event that could have sent her life into negative turmoil now impacts thousands of lives in a positive way.

Admit it, some of us wouldn't get back in the water after seeing the movie *Jaws*, let alone after losing an arm to a shark. Bethany could have easily changed her view of the world and decided to see it as dangerous and chaotic. She could have chosen to give up her love for surfing in order to protect herself from another attack. However, Bethany chose to embrace her fear and not allow it to take away the love and sense of adventure that she experiences riding the waves.

Have you been hurt in the past? Did you have a bad boss or get fired or fail in a major endeavor due to things outside of your control? Those experiences may have impacted your view of the workplace. There are many choices we have to make about how we see the world after such experiences. The first choice has to do with whether we see opportunities or problems.

Opportunities vs. Problems

Martha Washington said, "The greatest part of our happiness depends on our dispositions, not our circumstances." Do you believe this when challenges come your way? When facing difficulties, do you focus on the problems or on the opportunities waiting to be born? Those who choose to focus on the problems usually feel threatened, discouraged, or controlled by the world. They complain about the problems rather than finding the unique angle that will turn those lemons into lemonade. Others embrace the challenge and work diligently to make good come from the bad. Take the story of Lou Holtz, for example.

Despite achieving the best record in university history, in 1983 Lou Holtz was fired as head football coach of the University of Arkansas. Despite his disappointment Lou decided to be positive and focus on creating his future. Therefore, he did not make a public spectacle out of his unfair firing. Within a few years Lou applied to be the head coach at the University of Notre Dame. The athletic director did proper due diligence and called Lou's references, including the University of Arkansas. Lou's former boss gave him a glowing recommendation and focused on his positive attitude and graceful way that he left. He also confessed that firing Lou was a mistake. Of course, Lou went on to create a legendary career as head coach of Notre Dame.

What would have happened if Lou had made other choices, such as focusing on his unfair firing and letting it depress him, or publicly complaining? He likely would have failed to find the opportunity hiding right behind the challenge. Seeing opportunities even in the most difficult times allows top performers to excel from challenges rather than be crushed by them.

Marcus Aurelius teaches, "If you are distressed by anything external, the pain is not due to the thing itself, but to your estimate of it; and this you have the power to revoke at any moment." External challenges are given much of their power due to our choice to be frightened of them. The truth is that great fortune comes from times of discomfort. In fact, author M. Scott Peck said, "The truth is that our finest moments are most likely to occur when we are feeling deeply uncomfortable, unhappy, or unfulfilled. For it is only in such moments, propelled by our discomfort, that we are likely to step out of our ruts and start searching for different ways or truer answers." The discomfort of challenges has lead to incredible discoveries, advanced thinking, and stronger people. If we focus on opportunity, challenges stretch us instead of stress us. Martin Luther King, Jr. claimed that "The ultimate measure of a man is not where he stands in moments of comfort and convenience but where he stands at times of challenge." Challenge reveals and shapes our character. If we let it, challenge has the potential to take us to heights we have never previously achieved. Perhaps Maya Lin, the architect who designed the Vietnam Wall, captured it best with, "To fly, we have to have resistance." If our eyes are too focused on the problem, we will miss the opportunity. As Helen Keller, who was no stranger to dealing with things she could not control, puts it, "When one door of happiness closes, another opens; but often we look so long at the closed door that we do not see the one which has been opened for us."

Impacting vs. Blaming

So when these challenges come your way, who needs to change: you, or the world? When something is bothering you in the workplace or at home, do you sit and complain about how others (including the corporation) need to do things differently, or do you focus on what you need to do? Our society loves to blame. If you watch television news after any natural disaster, accident, or tragedy, the phrase "who is to blame" pops up with lightning speed. During the Hurricane Katrina tragedy I found myself wondering what more we could have accomplished if all the energy spent on blame was focused on rescuing people. Could we have saved one more life? Perhaps a dozen? When faced with difficulties, tragedies, or overwhelming circumstances, top performers do something about it rather than staying focused on what everyone else should be doing about it. Blame is tempting because it makes us feel superior to others. It also gives us an illusion of control. If we can find someone to blame, then we feel a false sense of control over things that frighten us.

In a corporate setting this translates into a "passing the buck" mentality. It's an unavoidable fact that things go wrong and sometimes we do not get the results we expect or are expected to get. What do you do when that happens? Those with a lesser attitude go immediately to a blaming mentality. Who's at fault? Who should have done better? Of course, it is wise to assess the causes of the problem in order to learn from it, but there is a time and a place for analysis and development. When something goes wrong, top performers immediately focus on what they can do to fix it. They change the situation rather than finding someone to blame for it. Analysis is done to correct the problem and increase performance, not to find blame and thus protect ego.

Paradoxically, a pattern of blaming does not really protect you. When you are focused on blaming others, you do not learn; and when you do not learn, you do not grow. Lack of growth means you are vulnerable to failure. Those who focus on what they can change about themselves and challenging situations get a reputation as go-to people who get results. They learn from every experience and get the outcomes needed to make the company stronger and more stable. Those who change instead of blame are the leaders who others respect and follow.

Tenacity vs. Abandonment

An attitude of tenacity is core to the top performer. Take the story of Bo Bishop, written by Catherine Madera in the September/October 2006 issue of *Positive Thinking*. Bo loved horses all of her life, and in 2001 started the process of turning her passion into a career. She was working on her horsemanship instructor's certification when a horse kicked her violently in the face. The article states that her nose was broken in "more than forty pieces," both of her eye sockets were damaged and her right eye was eventually lost, and her face had to be rebuilt "using tiny titanium screws." Most people would have seen this as a sign that their dream wasn't meant to be. Not Bo. All she could think of was getting on a horse again.

Within seven months Bo returned to her passion with greater commitment than ever before. Her final words in the article were, "I'm thankful every day." Bo has incredible tenacity.

A tenacious attitude is one of the best predictors of success. Top performers are individuals who love challenges—they view difficulties the same way that track runners see hurdles. They can't wait to jump over them! That is thrill of competition. Michael Jordan captures it well with, "Obstacles don't have to stop you. If you run into a wall, don't turn around and give up. Figure out how to climb it, go through it, or work around it." What do you do when you come to a hurdle? Do you stop and complain, or do you immediately start exploring ways to conquer the challenge?

Some people stay tenacious to the very end. In the 2006 November/December issue of *Mental Floss*, an article entitled "Would You Believe: Unbelievable Last Words" quoted the last words of French nobleman Thomas de Mahy. As revolutionaries handed him his official death sentence, he stayed defiant to the end. What were his last words? "I see that you have made three spelling mistakes." Defiance against all odds has inspired mankind across history. Whether it be

Napoleon's, "Circumstances—what are circumstances? I make circumstances"; or Hubert Humphrey stating, "Oh, my friend, it's not what they take away from you that counts. It's what you do with what you have left"; or Voltaire reminding us that "Life is a shipwreck, but we must not forget to sing in the lifeboats," we must always remember that greatness follows tenacity. Sometimes tenacity changes the world, but there are times when we are completely helpless to change the external world and must make a choice to embrace those things we cannot control.

Embracing vs. Resisting

Many individuals try to fight against uncontrollable circumstances—they complain or torture themselves, take the issues home with them, and lose time and sleep over situations they can do absolutely nothing about. In contrast, top performers learn to embrace that which they are unable to change. In a chapter of *A Psychology of Human Strengths*, Charles Carver and Michael Scheier discuss how giving up becomes a strength when facing insurmountable obstacles. When a challenge you're facing is larger than your capabilities, they list two choices:

- Give up effort, but stay committed to the goal.
- Disengage from the goal.

The first choice is a lousy one and only leads to feeling helpless. It is far better to separate from the goal and follow any of three positive alternatives:

- Choose an alternative path or higher-order goal.
- Form a new goal.
- Scale back your goal.

Each of these has the potential for positive outcomes. In contrast, if you fail to pick a new goal, you could end up aimless and empty. Embracing reality does not need to end in despair. Rather, it can end in additional, different, or even better goals than your original one. That is the very practical level of embracing, but it's also important on an emotional level. In *Tuesdays with Morrie: An Old Man, a Young Man, and Life's Greatest Lesson*, Mitch Albom writes, "Learn to detach. . . . Don't cling to things, because everything is impermanent. . . . But detachment doesn't mean you don't let the experience penetrate you. On the contrary, you let it penetrate fully. That's how you are able to leave it."

So the concept of embracing things we can't control does not mean that we deny, avoid, or run from them. In contrast, we turn, face, and fully accept them. Only then do they lose power. So if you're upset about that co-worker who annoys everyone (and you have tried to impact the situation with no results), it may just be time to accept that you have no control over it. Fully embrace that co-worker as annoying and ineffective. See the situation for what it is and then after fully feeling it, simply let go. No longer give it any power, because the more power you give it, the more pain you will feel. In *The Way of the Peaceful Warrior*, Dan Millman clearly emphasizes the relationship between resisting and pain. He writes, "Pain is a relatively objective, physical phenomenon; suffering is our psychological resistance to what happens. Events may create physical pain, but they do not in themselves create suffering. Resistance creates suffering. Stress happens when your mind resists what is. . . . The only problem in your life is your mind's resistance to life as it unfolds."

Of course, part of the trick is to distinguish between those situations you can control and those you cannot. Top performers do not ignore destructive coworkers if they can impact the situation. As John Wooden, arguably the greatest college basketball coach of all time, puts it, "Do not let what you cannot do interfere with what you can do." Taking responsibility and tenaciously working to impact situations is critical in order to have the attitude of a top performer. We only get into trouble when we become too invested in the world being one certain way, and that way only. When we believe there is only one path to happiness, we have developed a scarcity mentality.

Abundance vs. Scarcity

Look at the coworker to your right (peek out of your office if necessary), then look at the coworker to your left. Are there enough rewards and successes for all of you? The attitude decision of believing in abundance instead of scarcity will have a profound impact on how you operate within your corporation and within the world. Those who believe in scarcity show undesirable behaviors, such as keeping efficiency processes they have developed to themselves and hiding other successful strategies.

These behaviors do not serve the corporation and ultimately do not serve the individual. Since much of your attitude will be influenced by the success of the organization, any behaviors that hamper that success will hurt your positive feelings and attitude.

Another form of scarcity mentality is when you stay in a job that is wrong for you. In one of my first coaching sessions with a major Fortune 100 contract, I talked to one such individual. After one hour of a highly unusual coaching session, he decided to leave his job. Within two weeks he was gone, and I was dreading my discussion with the executive who hired me to coach this gentleman. To my delight he thanked me for my work saying, "The person you coached had been in the wrong position for ten years. It is about time he did something about it." Now compare that situation with my coaching of Daniel. He also was a square peg in a round hole at his job, and he fully knew it. However, it took him almost a year to leave because he was frightened that he could not find another good opportunity (and was afraid to even look). In that time he was miserable, and so was his boss. When he finally left, he quickly found his dream job and is happier now than he has ever been. Are there guarantees on any of this? Of course not, but your belief in abundant opportunities will have an impact on how many come your way. The abundant thinker believes that there is enough out there for all of us and there are many paths to fulfillment.

Gratitude vs. Entitlement

Anne Frank said, "I don't think of all the misery but of the beauty that still remains." What incredible words from someone who witnessed unfairness in life that most of us will likely never know. Despite her challenges she was still able to see the beauty in this world, and was grateful for it.

All three of your authors do significant work in the financial services industry. It is an amazing industry with many talented individuals who are making an incredible difference in the lives of their clients. It is also an industry fraught with the evils and dangers that come with money. Frequently in coaching sessions we run across someone who thinks he or she deserves to make more money. Now, we are not against making more money, and we have helped many clients do so. Money can be used for wonderful purposes. However, when someone making a hefty six-figure salary is bitter because he believes that he deserves to make more, then that person has lost sight of the world and his blessings. He has fallen into the quagmire of entitlement, and once you are in that quicksand it is very difficult to claw your way out of it.

True top performers live with a sense of gratitude. They live their days feeling appreciation for all that they have and all that they will have. Top performers have a larger worldview and realize that they have been blessed in ways unusual to most of the world's population (whether with money, talents, opportunities, etc.). Now, it doesn't mean that they feel satisfied. In our experience, top performers rarely feel satisfied. They are often looking for the next challenge and always striving to do better. *Satisfaction* and *gratitude* are two different concepts. Satisfaction implies fulfillment (and no need to continue pursuing new opportunities); gratitude just means an appreciation for what you have. So a top performer can (and often does) want more money, status, influence, or impact, but he or she does not confuse *want* with *deserves*. As Mark Twain put it, "Don't go around saying the world owes you a living. The world owes you nothing. It was here first." Entitlement is poison to the attitude of the top performer. Living in gratitude while we strive to create more gives us peace, strength, and the ability to focus on the future rather than mourn past regrets. When a top performer goes through tough times, they view the world differently. "I take nothing for granted.

I now have only good days or great days," said Lance Armstrong after his battle with cancer. This perspective is part of what makes him one of the best in his field.

Even in times of chaos, top performers are grateful because they search for purpose in the difficulties. By pursuing purpose they find purpose and, if nothing else, are grateful for the lessons learned. And gratitude is shown in how you live. John F. Kennedy said, "As we express our gratitude, we must never forget that the highest appreciation is not to utter words, but to live by them."

Together vs. Separate

One of the biggest complaints we get from our corporate clients is that managers and departments within the corporation get stuck in "silo mentalities." On a simplistic level, a silo mentality is an attitude of me versus them (although the *me* can also be a group you're in charge of if the group becomes a narcissistic representation of you). In one workshop, we spoke immediately after a human resources representative who gave a moving message to our up-and-coming participants about the destructive nature of silos. As he finished speaking about the need for the leaders to break through silo thinking, everyone applauded with enthusiasm and support for this powerful message. They were committed to breaking the silo thinking in the company. Following this message we spoke for about twenty minutes on

coaching skills for leaders, and then broke the participants into five groups and placed them in different areas
of the room in order to do a teamwork exercise. We gave
the groups instructions on the mock challenges they
were facing and told them that they were all part of the
same company and that they were in competition with an
outside company (not represented by anyone in the
room) that was working on the same project. We then
sent them back to their groups to work on five mental
challenges that were difficult (but not impossible) to
solve in the time frame we allowed. Each group had the
same five problems to solve.

At the end of fifteen minutes, no group had completed
more than three of the challenges correctly. We stopped
them and gave them the answers, then asked them how
they thought they did on their teamwork. They all felt
great about their groups until we asked them to repeat
back the instructions for the exercise. They could repeat
back everything we said except one phrase we snuck into
the instructions. The phase they could not remember and
did not act on was, "we are all in this together." You see,
none of the five groups worked with each other, even
though we told them they were all on the same team. Just
by separating them in the room, they automatically
created silos and did not work together. And of course the
kicker is that this happened just a few minutes after they
made a vow to break their silos.

The lesson? Silos form very easily and create an attitude of separateness, inappropriate competition, and lesser performance between talented groups. A collective mentality is hard to protect, but it is an attitude that top performers know is important in building a stable corporate powerhouse. The silo mentality creates vulnerability and the attitude of self-preservation. Many companies suffer from leaders who protect their turf at the sake of the good of the entire company. True top performers focus on the fact that together, you can accomplish far more than you can separate.

Interviews with Top Performers

Bo Carrington is a senior consultant for the Hayes Group International, Inc., and has more than sixteen years of experience working with leaders at all levels. He shared this about attitude: "The most helpful thing that I ever learned was that life is all about choices. Every day when we get up, we have a choice as to the attitude that we are going to adopt. We have a choice to make about how we are going to respond when attacked by someone else or the attitude we put on when under stress or trial. We protect it by constantly reminding ourselves that, in a world in which we have little true control, our attitude is one thing that no one other than ourselves has access to or control over." Like your authors, Bo believes that the choices you make about how you view and interact with the world will greatly impact your happiness, relationships, and effectiveness in being a top performer.

Putting It into Practice

Fill in the chart below to gain insight into the choices you are making daily about the world.

Attitudes about the world	What are some warning signs that you are falling into the negative choice?	What corrective actions can you do at those moments that will help you make the positive choice?
Opportunities vs. Problems		
Impacting vs. Blaming		
Tenacity vs. Abandonment		
Embracing vs. Resisting		
Abundance vs. Scarcity		
Gratitude vs. Entitlement		
Together vs. Separate		

SECTION III

DEVELOPING A TOP-PERFORMING ATTITUDE

CHAPTER 5

BUILD AN UNBREAKABLE ATTITUDE

Attitude Adages

Confidence is directness and courage in meeting the facts of life.
—Author John Dewey

A positive attitude may not solve all your problems, but it will annoy enough people to make it worth the effort.
—Herm Albright, quoted in *Reader's Digest*, June 1995

In a Nutshell

By now you have studied the concepts and explored the choices you must make in order to be a top performer. In this chapter, we will start looking at how to adopt them. We will explore the path to developing an unbreakable attitude and go through a step-by-step method for coaching yourself out of negativity and into the realm of possibilities.

It's All in How You Look at It

At avonlakeschools.com you can find a wonderful story about attitude. The story is about the manager of a restaurant in Philadelphia, Pennsylvania, named Jerry. According to the article, Jerry always shows a positive attitude. When someone asks how he is doing, he responds with "If I were any better, I would be twins!" When Jerry changes jobs and moves to a new restaurant, people quit and follow him. That is how inspirational he is. The writer of the article approached Jerry and asked him how he could have such a consistently great attitude. Jerry said, "Each morning I wake up and say to myself, I have two choices today: I can choose to be in a good mood or I can choose to be in a bad mood. I always choose to be in a good mood. Each time something bad happens, I can choose to be a victim or I can choose to learn from it. I always choose to learn from it. Every time someone comes to me complaining, I can choose to accept their complaining or I can point out the positive side of life. I always choose the positive side of life." The writer admits feeling skeptical about Jerry's viewpoint at the time.

Several years passed, and the writer heard that Jerry was robbed in his restaurant by three gunmen. Jerry was shot in the process and had to go through eighteen hours of surgery. The writer revisited Jerry six months later. When asked how he was, Jerry replied, "If I were any better, I'd be twins. Want to see my scars?" When asked about the robbery, this is what Jerry had to say: "The first thing that went through my mind was that I should have locked the back door. Then, after they shot me, as I lay on the floor, I remembered that I had two choices: I could choose to live or choose to die. I chose to live." At the hospital, as the doctors and nurses were frantically trying to help Jerry, they asked if he was allergic to anything. Jerry replied, "Yes, bullets." As they laughed, he informed them of his plan to live and asked for them to believe with him that he would be saved. The writer took this thought away from that meeting: "I learned from him that every day you have the choice to either enjoy your life or to hate it. The only thing that is truly yours—that no one can control or take from you—is your attitude, so if you can take care of that, everything else in life becomes much easier."

Once you fully embrace the fact that attitude is a choice, you simply have to follow a four-step process for taking control of it, and thus taking control of your life. We use the acronym of DO IT to capture these four steps.

- Determine the influences
- Organize your choices
  - Thoughts: Pick the perspectives and thoughts that will create a top performing attitude.
  - Emotions: Embrace and challenge your emotions.
  - Behaviors: Evaluate your possible actions.
- Influence the outcome (execute your strategy)
- Test your approach

Determine the Influences

It is important to determine how events and relationships from your present and past are impacting your attitude.

For example, if you were neglected by your parents in your childhood, you are more likely to see abandonment in your present (even when it may not exist). This could create a tendency to be self-protective. Even current relationships can set you up for subconscious attitude choices that do not serve you. For example, let's say you are recently divorced and your ex-spouse is taking you to the cleaners, so to speak, in the negotiations. It may be especially difficult to have an attitude of abundance during this time. Or let's consider your current work culture. If you are surrounded by takers and negativity, it will be difficult to have a positive and giving attitude. This is why this first step is so important: You must do an honest and thorough assessment of the external factors that could potentially be impacting your attitude. Know the playing field and don't be so naive as to think you are 100% immune to these current or past influences. The best way to determine what is influencing you is to watch for patterns in your life. What reoccurring themes do you keep experiencing? These will give you a great start in determining what is influencing your thinking, emotions, and behaviors.

Organize Your Thinking, Emotional, and Behavioral Choices

Once you have determined your influences, it's time to organize your choices. We have identified twenty-one attitude choices throughout this book that you can make about yourself, other people, and the world. Now is the time to apply these by looking at your thoughts, emotions, and actions.

External factors are highly susceptible to your interpretation and perspectives. Two people can work with the exact same boss and have two completely different views of the person. Top performers take control of these thoughts. Here are a few questions to ask yourself that can help you positively realign your thoughts in any situation:

- What is the best way to view this situation?
- If I were to give everyone the benefit of the doubt in this situation, how would I see it?
- What perspective can I take that will create a top-performing attitude?
- What do I choose to believe about myself, others, and the world in this situation?

Emotions play an equally important role in your attitude. Ask these questions to help challenge or (if your feelings are based on truth) embrace your emotions:

- What am I feeling? And if that feeling is anger, what do I feel beneath the anger? (Many times we feel hurt, embarrassed, frustrated, shamed, fearful, etc. beneath anger, and dealing with these core emotions helps us.)

- How much of what I feel is due to how I am choosing to interpret what happened?
- What do I choose to feel about myself, others, and the world in this situation?

Once your thoughts and emotions are within your control, your behaviors are likely to follow. Attitude is evidenced by your behaviors—you can't claim to have an attitude of forgiveness and continue to talk badly about someone. You can't claim to have an attitude of *we* when your behaviors continue to be *me* focused. Some self-coaching questions concerning behaviors are:

- What are my choices of how to respond to this situation?
- What action will likely get the most productive result?
- How do I choose to act with integrity toward myself, others, and the world in this situation?

With each of these areas you will want to review the twenty-one choices presented in this book and make sure you are on the top-performing side of the equation. By organizing your thoughts, emotions, and action choices, you are claiming control over your life rather than letting life claim control over you. Once you have organized your choices, it is time to execute them.

Influence the Outcome (Execute Your Strategy)

We use the word *influence* deliberately here. Remember that, often, you may not have complete control over the outcome of a situation—and we are not suggesting that a positive attitude will guarantee that every single dream you have will come true in every single way you want it to. However, we confidently claim that an optimistic attitude will greatly increase your chances of getting a great outcome. And attitude without action is not truly a top-performing attitude—you need to follow through on your positive thoughts, feelings, and action choices. Make them happen! When you execute on your positive attitude, the absolute worst-case scenario is that you will not be able to change the situation, but you will have the peace of knowing that you did all you could do. Then you can remove any self-inflicted pain by choosing to embrace the situation instead of resisting it.

Some self-coaching questions to ask yourself are:

- How tenacious do I want to be in pursuing my goal?
- What can't I control (what do I need to embrace about the challenge)?
- What higher, scaled back, or different goals would be better to pursue?

Test Your Approach

After influencing the outcome, top performers review and assess their actions—they rewind the tape and evaluate their performance in order to improve their game. They assess what did and what did not work about their approach. They learn from every trial and continue to perfect their attitude and their behaviors for the rest of their lives. Therefore, the last stage in our DO IT process is to test your approach. To do this you can ask the following questions:

- How well did my approach work?
- What did I do well in my strategy?
- If I could do it all over again, what would I tweak or change?

Pride can cause a person to say such things as "I did the best I could" or "I am what I am." Top performers would not be caught dead with these excuses. They are confident enough to put their actions to the test and humble enough to see ways to grow and improve.

Determine the influences, organize your choices, influence the outcome, and test your strategies—these steps will put you on a path to capturing the attitude of a top performer. As my pastor once said, "It is not rocket science; it is just hard." With wisdom and effort you can become a master at accepting your personal power, interacting positively with others, and seeing the world as a place of opportunity and a testing ground to grow your knowledge, abilities, and perspective.

Twenty-One Choices

This book is about the choices you make regarding your personal power, your relationships, and how you interact with the world. We have covered twenty-one different choices that you can make. Our hope is that you will choose the following.

About yourself

- Hoping over being helplessness
- Pursuing your potential over stagnating
- Owning your life instead of feeling like a victim
- Acting out of conviction instead of shame
- Venting instead of whining
- Dreaming when you are tempted to doubt
- Building a future rather than obsessing about the past

About others

- Focusing on others' strengths instead of their flaws
- Accepting others instead of judging them
- Being open and vulnerable instead of protected and closed
- Confronting issues, not avoiding them
- Giving more than you take
- Forgiving others instead of holding on to hurts

- Delivering what you promise so you won't disappoint others

About the world

- Finding those opportunities that hide in the problems
- Impacting the things you can control rather than blaming others
- Being tenacious and persistent even when you feel like giving up
- Embracing those things that are bigger than you and that you can't control
- Taking an abundance mentality instead of believing in scarcity
- Living in gratitude rather than feeling entitled
- Having a mentality of togetherness and not getting trapped in your little silo

The astute reader will notice that these were the same choices we had you assess yourself on in our first chapter. Twenty-one choices—could twenty-one choices change your life? Could twenty-one choices help you create amazing relationships and results and protect you from any curve ball this world could throw you? If you answered a resounding yes, then we have done our job.

Interviews with Top Performers

One of our favorite top performers is a man named Barry Foster. Barry is the president of Fostering Solutions, Inc.; the CEO of ASearch, LLC; and the founder/director of the Corporate Coaching Center. Barry sees attitude as the "keystone to other qualities such as character, courage, integrity, initiative, passion, and commitment." He puts effort into cultivating his attitude by beginning each day with readings from positive and motivating writers. Barry believes this sets the tone for his day. Friends and colleagues call Barry the "eternal optimist," and he accepts that title with appropriate pride. One of the reasons that Barry has done so well is that he focuses on action. In our interview, Barry revealed his strong beliefs: "To me, just saying, 'look at the bright side' of a situation or circumstance is not enough. One has to be willing to follow that up with positive action. Do something constructive about it instead of looking at the destructive side of a situation." I know Barry well, and I can guarantee that he is a man of action. Despite being the leader of several organizations and someone that others come to for guidance, Barry invests in having his own coach. Despite doing well and being justified at taking life easy, he works hard and always gives his clients his best. Despite being respected as a top performer, he never stops challenging himself to go to the next level. He says,

"When is continuous improvement done? Never! I always look at ways I can learn and improve how I do what I do." And then Barry reminded me of a quote that I have heard him say many times, "The only place success comes before work is in the dictionary."

The Time for Action

Lots of people read books, but top performers do more than read; top performers take action. If this book has spoken to you in any way, then it is time to make these choices your own. One of the best ways to truly live these choices is to teach them to others. So share whichever concepts touched you with those around you. Practice your attitude choices daily, and live the life of a top performer. We started this book out by asking you a question: "Can a book truly change your life?" The full truth is that a book can help, but only you can change your life. You have amazing abilities and talents, and we hope that this little book helps motivate you to make the top-performing choices that we know you can make. Claim those thoughts, emotions, and actions that will make your life joyful, your relationships fulfilling, and your perform-ance go through the roof. Spend the rest of your life with the attitude of a top performer.

BIBLIOGRAPHY

Albom, Mitch. *Tuesdays with Morrie*. New York: Doubleday, 2005.

Allen, James. *As a Man Thinketh*. Kansas City: Andrews McMeel Publishing, n.d.

Aspinwall, Lisa G., and Ursula M. Staudinger. *A Psychology of Human Strengths*. Washington, DC: American Psychological Association, 2002.

Buckingham, Marcus, and Dr. Donald O. Clifton. *Now, Discover Your Strengths*. New York: Free Press, 2001.

Chen, N. "Individual Differences in Answering the Four Questions for Happiness." PhD diss., University of Georgia–Athens, 1996.

Collins, Jim. *Good to Great*. N.p.: Collins, 2001.

Craste, Michele, David Barlow, and Tracy O'Leary. *Mastery of Your Anxiety and Worry*. N.p.: Oxford University Press, 1991.

Fillmore, Charles. *12 Powers of Man*. N.p.: Unity School of Christianity, 1995.

"Gallup Study: Feeling Good Matters in the Work Place." *Gallup Management Journal*, January 2006.

Glass, D. C. *Urban Stress*. New York City: Academic Press, 1972.

Hamilton, Bethany. "Teen Shark Victim: Can't Wait to Surf Again." Interviewed by Bill Hemmer. *CNN* 25 (Jan. 2003). http://www.cnn.com/2003/US/11/25/cnna.hamilton/ (accessed May 19, 2007).

Hill, Napoleon. *Think and Grow Rich*. San Diego: Aventine Press, 2004.

Lopez, Shane J., and C. R. Snyder. *Positive Psychological Assessment*. Washington, DC: American Psychological Association, 2003.

Maddi, S.R., D.M. Khoshaba, and A. Pammenter. "The Hardy Organization: Success by Turning Change to Advantage." *Consulting Psychology Journal*. 51 (1999): 117-124.

Madera, Catherine. "Love Your Life." *Positive Thinking*, September 2006, 60–61.

Maxwell, John C. *Real Leadership: The 101 Collection*. Nashville, TN: Thomas Nelson, Inc., 2003.

Millman, Dan. *Way of the Peaceful Warrior*. Tiburon, CA: HJ Kramer, 1980.

Niven, Dr. David. *The 100 Simple Secrets of Happy People*. New York City: HarperCollins Publishers, 2000.

Peale, Norman Vincent. *The Power of Positive Thinking*. N.p.: Running Press Book Publishers, 2002.

"The Progenitors of Positivity." *Newsweek*, March 2007.

Robertson, Kelley. "High Income Seller Behaviors." *Selling*, October 2005, 14.

Seligman, Dr. Martin. *Authentic Happiness: Using the New*

THE TOP PERFORMER'S GUIDE TO ATTITUDE

Positive Psychology to Realize Your Potential for Lasting Fulfillment. New York City: Free Press, 2002.

Shawshank Redemption. Directed by Frank Darabont. Warner Home Video, 1994.

Stein, Dr. Steven J., and Dr. Howard E. Book. *The EQ Edge.* Toronto: Stoddart Publishing Co. Limited, 2000.

Sugarman, S. "Happiness and Population Density." Master's thesis, California State University–Long Beach, 1997.

Turner, T. J. "Basic Emotions: Can Conflicting Criteria Converge?" *Psychological Review* (1992): 566–571.

Wattles, Wallace. *The Science of Getting Rich.* Inala Heights, Queensland, Australia: KT Publishing, 2005.

Williams, A., D. Haber, G. Weaver, and J. Freeman. "Altruistic Activity." *Activities, Adaptation, and Aging* 22 (1998): 31.

"Would You Believe: Unbelievable Last Words." *Mental Floss*, November/December 2006, 22.

INDEX

D

T

ABOUT THE
AUTHORS

Tim Ursiny, PhD, the founder of Advantage Coaching & Training, is a success coach specializing in human behavior and achievement in life and in the workplace. He is an expert on communication skills and conflict resolution. Before becoming one of the leading personal and business coaches in the country, he was a psychologist in private practice for seven years. He has authored and coauthored multiple books, including *The Coward's Guide to Conflict*, *The Confidence Plan*, *Coaching the Sale*, and many books in the *Top Performer's* series. You can reach Tim at Drtim@advantagecoaching.com.

Gary DeMoss is director of Van Kampen Consulting, which provides communication and relationship skills training to financial advisors. Gary is a keynote speaker, seminar leader, and consultant to advisors who want to build their affluent client base, and he was recently selected as a platform speaker at the 2003 Million Dollar Round Table conference. He is the coauthor of the books *Coaching the Sale*, *The Top Performer's Guide to Presentations*, and *The Financial Professional's Guide to*

Persuading 1 or 1,000. You can reach Gary at demossg@ vankampen.com.

Marc A. Ybaben, PhD, is a consulting psychologist, and has been an executive coach with Advantage Coaching & Training since 2000. He is a sought-after speaker and trainer, and specializes in individual and organizational performance enhancement projects. Marc is an expert in the assessment, selection, and development of leaders for emerging companies, and you can reach him at marcwhy@earthlink.net.